A Den for Bei Bei

Joseph Otterman

✳ Smithsonian

trees

hammock

rocks

grass

mural

snow

ball

cameras

STEAM CHALLENGE

The Problem

Bei Bei needs a hammock! Can you build him one?

The Goals

- Your hammock should be small for a stuffed animal.
- Use any materials you like. Be sure to hang the hammock so both ends are off the ground.
- Test the hammock with a stuffed animal. It should hold for at least two minutes.

Research and Brainstorm

Learn about Bei Bei.

Design and Build

Draw your plan. Build your hammock!

Test and Improve

Put a stuffed animal in the hammock. Then, try to make it better.

Reflect and Share

What did you learn?

Consultants

Amy Zoque
STEM Coordinator and Instructional Coach
Vineyard STEM School
Ontario Montclair District

Siobhan Simmons
Marblehead Elementary
Capistrano Unified School District

Publishing Credits

Rachelle Cracchiolo, M.S.Ed., *Publisher*
Conni Medina, M.A.Ed., *Editor in Chief*
Diana Kenney, M.A.Ed., NBCT, *Series Developer*
Emily R. Smith, M.A.Ed., *Content Director*
Véronique Bos, *Creative Director*
Robin Erickson, *Art Director*
Stephanie Bernard, *Associate Editor*
Mindy Duits, *Senior Graphic Designer*
Smithsonian Science Education Center

Image Credits: front cover, p.1, p.3, p.18, p.20 © Smithsonian; p.7, p.11 Rebecca Hale/National Geographic; p.9 Tim Brown/Alamy; p.13 Ann Batdorf/Smithsonian's National Zoo; p.15 AP Photo/Jose Luis Magana; p.17 Matt McClain/The Washington Post via Getty Images; all other images from Shutterstock.

Library of Congress Cataloging-in-Publication Data

Names: Otterman, Joseph, 1964- author.
Title: A den for Bei Bei / Joseph Otterman.
Description: Huntington Beach, CA : Teacher Created Materials, Inc., [2020] | Audience: Age 5. | Audience: K to Grade 3. |
Identifiers: LCCN 2018055255 (print) | LCCN 2018056469 (ebook) | ISBN 9781425859763 (eBook) | ISBN 9781493866311 (paperback)
Subjects: LCSH: Giant panda--Housing--Juvenile literature. | Zoo animals--Juvenile literature. | Hammocks--Juvenile literature.
Classification: LCC QL737.C27 (ebook) | LCC QL737.C27 O89 2020 (print) | DDC
 599.789156/4--dc23
LC record available at https://lccn.loc.gov/2018055255

✺ **Smithsonian**

© 2019 Smithsonian Institution. The name "Smithsonian" and the Smithsonian logo are registered trademarks owned by the Smithsonian Institution.

Teacher Created Materials

5301 Oceanus Drive
Huntington Beach, CA 92649-1030
www.tcmpub.com
ISBN 978-1-4938-6631-1
© 2019 Teacher Created Materials, Inc.
Printed in Malaysia
Thumbprints.21248